World's Most Spine-Tingling "True" Ghost Stories

Sheila Anne Barry

Illustrated by Jim Sharpe

Sterling Publishing Co., Inc.   New York

Library of Congress Cataloging-in-Publication Data

Barry, Sheila Anne.
   World's most spine-tingling "true" ghost stories / by Sheila Anne
Barry ; illustrated by Jim Sharpe.
      p.   cm.
   Includes index.
   ISBN 0-8069-8686-7.—ISBN 0-8069-8687-5 (pbk.)
    1. Ghosts—Juvenile literature. I. Sharpe, Jim. II. Title.
BF1461.B377   1992
133.1—dc20   92-19862
                                  CIP
                                  AC

To my teacher, Joseph Lukach,
with love and gratitude

10 9 8 7 6 5 4 3 2 1

Published in 1992 by Sterling Publishing Company, Inc.
387 Park Avenue South, New York, N.Y. 10016
Text © 1992 by Sheila Anne Barry
Illustrations © 1992 by Jim Sharpe
Distributed in Canada by Sterling Publishing
% Canadian Manda Group, P.O. Box 920, Station U
Toronto, Ontario, Canada M8Z 5P9
Distributed in Great Britain and Europe by Cassell PLC
Villiers House, 41/47 Strand, London WC2N 5JE, England
Distributed in Australia by Capricorn Link Ltd.
P.O. Box 665, Lane Cove, NSW 2066
Manufactured in the United States of America
All rights reserved

Sterling ISBN 0-8069-8686-7 (hard)
               0-8069-8687-5 (paperback)

CONTENTS

1. INCREDIBLE!

- The mysterious disappearance of a young man takes place almost before the eyes of his horrified family.

- Two men's lives are linked—a king's and a commoner's—and so are their deaths.

- A prayer meeting becomes a scene of ultimate horror.

- Could a name save you from drowning? Try this one!

- A woman in despair is saved by her brother—thousands of miles away.

The Strange Disappearance of Charles Ashmore

Charles Ashmore was 16 years old on the November evening that he stepped outside his home to get some water from the well. He never came back.

It happened in Quincy, Illinois, in 1878. His father and sister went out looking for him with a lantern. They followed his footprints easily in the thin layer of snow that had just fallen. About halfway to the well, the footprints stopped. There was no sign of a struggle or a fall or even a jump or slide. They just stopped.

Really frightened now, the two hurried to the well. It was covered with ice—ice that had been frozen solid for hours. There was no chance that he had fallen in.

His father and sister, mystified, returned home where the family waited, desperate to have some answer to the puzzle. None came.

For days, Charles' mother walked back and forth along his route from the house to the well, hoping to find some clue to his disappearance.

On the fourth day, she heard her son's voice calling to her. She had been out by the well, but the voice wasn't coming from there. It would come from different directions—sometimes from above, sometimes from the sides. It sounded clear enough, but Charles wasn't there.

"Charlie, where are you? Tell us how to get to you," Mrs. Ashmore kept saying.

But she never got an answer to her questions.

For months afterwards at various times, Charles' voice was heard by other members of the family and by neighbors. It seemed to be coming from a greater distance away, but no one could identify the direction.

Gradually, the voice grew fainter, and by the middle of the summer, no one could hear it at all.

What happened to Charles Ashmore? Did he step into another dimension of time or space? Was he there all the time—beyond reach—unable to find his way home? If not, where did he go?

The Time Twins

King Umberto I of Italy had been told how amazingly one of his subjects resembled him, but he didn't really believe it until he walked into the restaurant the man owned and actually saw him.

It wasn't only a physical resemblance.

They also had the same first name.

They were born on the same day.

They had both always lived in the same town.

And, they married women with the same first names.

The man was a restaurant keeper, but he seemed as content with that as the king was with his crown.

The king invited the man to be the royal guest at a sports competition to be held the next day.

When the restaurant keeper didn't show up, the king was annoyed and sent one of his servants to find out why.

The king's man returned to report that the man had been shot that very morning and had died immediately.

Minutes later an assassin managed to get past the security guards and shoot Umberto I. He died at once.

The Wedding Ring

Ever since her husband, Charley, had been sent over-seas to serve as a bomber pilot, Betty Rae S_____ of Jackson, Mississippi, had stayed home listening to the radio and staring at Charley's picture. She only went out for groceries or to the church across the street where she prayed for Charley. She never missed a chance to pray for Charley.

One night, she woke to hear church bells ringing. It was after midnight. She got up and looked out the window. The church was all lit up and she could hear the congregation singing.

She was irritated as she hurried into her clothes. Saturday night was a weird time to call a prayer meeting, but she would have gone if she'd known about it. And how come the whole town knew about this one and Reverend Hawkins never told her?

Betty Rae rushed into the church and sat quickly in one of the pews. It wasn't Reverend Hawkins up there at the pulpit, but whoever it was, he could certainly offer up a good sermon.

It was odd, she thought, looking around, that she didn't recognize any of the people in the church. Probably it was a visiting evangelist and these people must be his followers.

Someone handed Betty Rae the collection plate. But, in her rush, she hadn't brought any money with her. She took the plate and passed it to the woman on her right.

"No, sister," the usher said loudly. "You didn't put anything in the plate."

"I didn't bring any money," Betty Rae said, "I'm really sorry."

"I'm sorry, too," the usher said unpleasantly, "but you've got to put something in the plate."

People began turning around and gawking at her.

"What's the trouble there, Brother Sam?" asked the preacher from the pulpit.

"This sister doesn't want to put anything in the plate," the usher said.

"Sister," the preacher bellowed, "you've got to put something in the plate!"

The church was buzzing.

"What can I do?" Betty Rae said. "I have nothing with me."

"You have your wedding ring," the usher said. "Put that in the plate."

"No—no!" Betty Rae screamed. "I can't do that!"

"Put the ring in the plate, Sister," thundered the preacher.

"Put the ring in the plate! Put the ring in the plate!" the congregation was chanting.

All eyes were on her. Betty Rae was trembling. She pulled the ring off her finger and dropped it in the collection plate. And suddenly she was filled with despair beyond anything she had ever known.

"Betty Rae, Betty Rae!" It was Reverend Hawkins' voice. He was bending down and looking into her face. "What are you doing here?"

Betty Rae straightened up. "Oh, this is terrible!" she shuddered. "I must have fallen asleep at the prayer meeting!"

"What prayer meeting?" said the Reverend Hawkins. "And how in the world did you get in here? I locked up yesterday afternoon and just unlocked the door this morning."

Betty Rae explained to Reverend Hawkins what had happened, and she was in tears again as she talked about the ring.

Reverend Hawkins went up to the front of the church and brought back one of the collection plates. There, sticking to the felt on the bottom of the plate, was her ring.

Monday morning, Betty Rae received the telegram that informed her that Charley had been killed when his plane went down over the English Channel. It must have happened at just about the time Betty Rae put her wedding ring in the collection plate.

Survivors of Tragedy

SHIPWRECKS

December 5, 1660	in the Straits of Dover	survivors: 1
December 5, 1781	in the Straits of Dover	survivors: 1
August 5, 1820	on the Thames	survivors: 1
July 10, 1940	in the Atlantic	survivors: 2

The amazing thing about this list of tragedies at sea is that all the survivors were named Hugh Williams—even the two who survived the 1940 sinking of a British trawler by a German mine. They were uncle and nephew—*both* named Hugh Williams.

Valentine's Visit

It was Valentine's Day and 18-year-old Teresa was in despair. On February 12th she had received an eviction notice from the tiny apartment she shared with her mother, who had died two weeks before. And she found herself unable to do anything about it.

She couldn't get herself to go into her mother's room, much less go through her things. She couldn't find a mover—on such short notice—who would move her from Baltimore to her uncle's house in Washington, D.C., 38 miles away, and her uncle was an old man who could not be of much help. Teresa had always been a sickly, solitary person, so there were no friends she could call upon.

If only Jimmy were here, she thought, he could take care of everything. Jimmy was her brother who was serving in Vietnam, and he hadn't been heard from for a long time. The Red Cross had tried to bring him home for the funeral, but it seemed that they were unsuccessful. They did report, however, that he had been notified of his mother's death.

Suddenly, as Teresa sat on the couch with her hands over her face, Jimmy was in the room—handsome as always and in uniform—the Red Cross must have succeeded after all!

What happened then seemed like a dream.

Jimmy went into their mother's bedroom with Teresa and helped her pack the things. Then he brought her back into the living room and told her to call a mover.

"I tried," Teresa told him, "and no one would do it."

"Try again," Jimmy said.

This time Teresa found a mover who had just had a cancellation and could do the moving that very day.

While they waited for the movers to come, Teresa and Jimmy packed up the few possessions in the apartment—without saying a word.

Then, when the movers arrived, Jimmy took Teresa by the shoulders and said, "You go with the truck, and don't look back. Do what Mother always wanted you to do, and remember, I'll always be with you."

When Teresa boarded the moving truck, the men asked her why her brother wasn't coming along to Washington.

"I guess he had to get back," she said, wondering about that herself.

It wasn't until the 10th of March, 1964, that Teresa found out why Jimmy had to get back. Because she received a telegram, forwarded from her old address, telling her that her brother had been killed in Vietnam on February 14th—the same day that he was with her.

2. CURSES, JINXES & BAD LUCK

- A Connecticut village is abandoned to the owls.

- A jinxed ring survives the accidents, disasters, and deaths of all its owners.

- An elegant pair of earrings has heavy luck-changing power—for good and evil.

- A malevolent submarine relentlessly kills workmen and crew.

- An African lake kills those who disturb it.

Village of the Cursed

Surrounded by mountains—so that even on a sunny day it lay in shadow—Dudleytown was once a thriving town in the county of Cornwall, Connecticut. Today it is overgrown and abandoned, left to the owls that earned it its nickname, "Owlsbury."

Some say the town was haunted. Others say there was a curse on it. But nobody lives there anymore. Some people don't even want to go near it. What happened?

Word has it that the bad luck of the town dates back to the Dudley family in England. Two of the Dudleys—nobles themselves—got into some serious trouble with the King and were beheaded. A third, returning from France, brought the plague back with him. Then a fourth, the Earl of Leicester, left England forever. It was his descendants who travelled to Connecticut to establish the New World branch of the family.

Two of them, Abiel and Barzillai, were the first Dudleys in Dudleytown in the 1700s. Perhaps the first case of bad luck was Abiel Dudley himself, who finished his days demented, as a ward of the state. His neighbor was also unlucky. While he lived to be 104, he was half crazy in his later years, they said, ever since a murder took place at his home.

Then there were a few epidemics that seemed to single out Dudleytown citizens, and a couple of mysterious ailments.

A Revolutionary War hero, General Herman Swift, went out of his mind when one of his wives was struck by lightning in an April storm.

Dudleytown native Mary Cheney, who married the famous journalist Horace Greeley, committed suicide shortly before her husband's defeat in a Presidential race. He died soon afterwards.

Young people left Dudleytown and did not return. That wasn't surprising—the land was rocky and infertile and high winds blew away the topsoil. There were few jobs. Older residents—the few who were left—moved out too.

Soon only one family was left. Patrick Brophy, his wife and his sons, had no intention of leaving Dudleytown. But then Brophy's two sons were caught stealing and ran off before the police could arrest them. Mrs. Brophy died of tuberculosis. And then the Brophy house burned down. Patrick Brophy finally just quit. And that was the end. Well, not quite. The strangest part of the story is yet to come.

Dr. William C. Clark, a professor in a New York medical school, fell in love with Dudleytown. He and his wife bought a tract of land to build on. No local builders were willing to work in the town, so, while visiting during the summers, the Clarks built their dream house with their own hands. They spent summer after summer happily in Dudleytown, and it seemed as if the curse was finally laid to rest.

Then one day, Dr. Clark was called to New York on a medical emergency. His wife saw him off at the station, obviously very sad to see him go.

Clark finished his work quickly and was back at the Cornwall station within 36 hours. But his wife wasn't there to meet him.

Filled with foreboding, he walked past the main path, Dark Entry Road, and through the woods to his summer cottage. The door was ajar. And then he heard sounds that made his blood run cold. It was his wife laughing—a hideous, horrible, crazy laugh. In his absence, she had gone completely mad.

Eventually, she committed suicide.

Dr. Clark was the last inhabitant to leave Dudleytown. Now only the owls remain. . . .

The Turquoise Ring

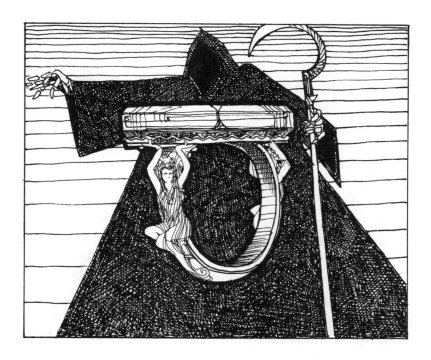

The ring was made in 1913. It was 14-carat gold with a square turquoise stone held in place by two beautifully sculpted nymphs. It was bought by Captain Albrecht Halberstern of the 11th Saxon Artillery Regiment, who sent the ring to his wife in Dresden. He went on to survive three years of combat on the Western Front, earned the Iron Cross, and returned home in November 1918. His wife had been killed the day before, while wearing the ring. She was hit through the temple by a stray bullet when she went out on her balcony—the only person to be killed in Dresden that day.

The ring was sold to a jeweler named Pecht. Soon after buying it, he went bankrupt and drowned himself.

Meanwhile, Captain Halberstern was feeling sentimental about his wife's jewelry. He bought back the ring, planning to wear it himself. He was wearing it when he went out riding in June 1929; his horse threw him and his injuries left him paralyzed and in a wheelchair.

After Hitler came to power, the Halberstern family was sent to Auschwitz. The Captain never made it all the way. His body was thrown from a cattle car with the dead.

The turquoise ring was rescued, however. It found its way into the possession of a Nazi labor front functionary named Kurt Weichter. He gave the ring to his wife on their 20th wedding anniversary and then his work took him to Czechoslovakia. He missed the infamous air attack on Dresden in which his wife, his parents, two children, and their dog were killed.

The turquoise ring survived the firestorm. It was the only possession Weichter had when the war ended. He sold it to a U.S. Army sergeant for 12 cartons of Lucky Strike cigarettes. He told the soldier it was a good luck charm.

The sergeant gave the ring to his fiancée, who gave it back when the engagement was broken off a month later. The sergeant's fingers were too thick to wear the ring, so he put it on a chain and wore it around his neck. He was wearing it on his wedding day when he and his new bride were driving out on a honeymoon trip to Lake Superior. His car collided with a truck at 70 miles per hour. Both the sergeant and his wife were killed instantly. The ring wasn't even dented. It went to his sister Caroline.

Caroline managed to wear the ring for six years without incident. Then her home was burgled by a young man named Robert Saugasso. He died not long afterwards, soon after falling—or being pushed—out a window. In his room, the police found the ring and returned it to Caroline.

Caroline was getting uncomfortable about the ring and tried to sell it. Not soon enough. Her marriage broke up and she was left with two young children and a husband who seldom paid child support. She finally sold the ring to an antique dealer named Landau.

The ring stayed in Landau's window for a year. The shop burned down. The ring was fine. Landau had a heart attack and died. His stock was auctioned off.

That's the last anyone knows of the turquoise ring. If you see it—a gold ring with nymphs and a big square stone—in a jeweler's window or at an auction or estate sale—beware.

The Greenstone Earrings

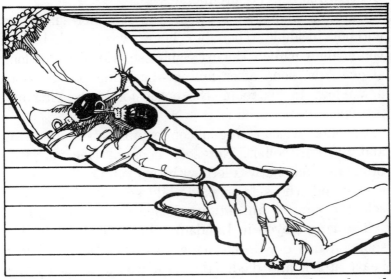

Leah was beautiful, highly educated and cultured, and part Maori—the race of native people who live in New Zealand. But she was not one to believe in the old Maori ways or follow the ancient traditions.

In time, however, when life became hard for Leah— with marriage troubles, little children to bring up, and no money—her mother handed down the family treasure, a pair of dark, glistening, pear-shaped greenstone earrings, which had been handed down for generations from mother to daughter. The earrings were said to be magical—instant luck changers and protectors—but they were also *tapu*—endowed with strange, inexplicable powers that were not to be taken lightly. They had to be treated with care and in accord with Maori laws. *Never* were they to pass out of the family. If no one was alive to inherit them, they were to be buried with their owner.

When Leah got the earrings, her life changed immediately. Within three months her divorce went through, she remarried, and she was enormously happy.

So when she saw her dear friend Dorothy Crombie, who had moved away from Rotorua to live in Auckland, she impulsively pressed the magnificent earrings into her hand.

"Take these," she said, "with my thanks for all the help you gave me during the bad times. May they bring you the wonderful luck that they have brought me."

That same day an accident happened.

Leah's youngest daughter, aged two, had been playing on the floor when a large pair of scissors somehow detached themselves from the nail they'd been hanging on and sailed across the room, striking the child just above the nose. She still has the scars.

The whole family started getting sick. Leah's oldest son, Wayne, was first diagnosed as having appendicitis. But instead, the problem turned out to be a large growth in his abdomen that returned after every operation removed it, baffling the doctors. He was not expected to recover.

When Leah's friend Dorothy heard about these difficulties, she determined to return the earrings, but she was told that she had to return them the same way she'd gotten them—by placing them in the hands. And Leah lived too far away.

Dorothy took up the earrings and spoke to them.

"I promise you that you will go home," she told the earrings, "when I return to Rotorua in just a few months."

As she spoke, the earrings went translucent for a moment, as if there were light held behind them, and then they turned to the side, showing their edges. When Dorothy told Maori friends about this later, they said, yes, that the earrings were telling her they were pleased to go home; they would do this only once.

Soon after that Dorothy received a note from Leah, asking for the earrings back. Evidently, things were getting worse and worse.

Dorothy and her husband got back to Rotorua within two weeks. When they arrived, Leah would not take the earrings back herself. Because she had given them away, she said, they were no longer hers. Dorothy could only give them to Leah's eldest daughter, Marion, who was six at the time.

Dorothy noticed that one of Marion's eyes was twisted. This disease, Leah had found out, was part of the *tapu*, and it would have travelled through the family until everyone had died—if the earrings had not been returned.

Leah also reported that an hour after she received Dorothy's telegram, she heard from the hospital that her son, Wayne, had recovered. He was now home with them all.

Wayne proudly showed his scars. They were wide apart—in the shape of a pair of earrings.

The Jinx and the Haunting of U-Boat 65

There are plenty of stories about haunted ships and bad luck ships, but the tale of U-boat 65 makes them all pale. It started in 1916. While the submarine was still under construction, a steel girder slid sideways and fell on two workmen. One was killed instantly. The other took an hour to die.

When U-boat 65 was almost ready for launching and workmen were putting finishing touches to the engine room equipment, poisonous fumes filled the cabin. The men tried to get out but the door was jammed. Three men choked to death. Why did the fumes escape? No one knew. Why did the door jam? No one knew. But Germany needed U-boats. The ship was deemed seaworthy.

When she went out for her trials, a member of the crew was swept overboard and drowned.

On her first test dive, the ship went down fine, but could not come up. A leak had developed in one of the tanks. She was down on the bottom for 12 hours. Once again poisonous fumes filled the ship, but they were able to bring her up before anyone died. Why couldn't the ship surface? No one could figure that out.

New trials were run and she was reported operational.

As the torpedoes were being loaded, one exploded. The toll? Six men, including Richter, the U-boat's second lieutenant.

That was the jinx—12 victims. Now for the haunting.

Before the ship started on her first war patrol, one of the enlisted men claimed that he had seen the second lieutenant—Richter, the one who had been killed—at the bow. Others had seen him too. The men were sworn to secrecy for fear of what a ghost rumor would do to morale.

Then, several days later, Richter was seen again at the bow, this time by the lookouts and the first lieutenant. He called the captain, who saw him also. Then the phantom vanished.

U-Boat 65 had barely docked at Bruges Navy Yard when air-raid sirens started screaming. The captain—on his way to shelter—was struck by a shell fragment that severed his head from his body. And at that very moment, several of the men standing in the shelter saw the figure of Richter at the bow of the ship.

By now, morale was nonexistent on the ship. The admiral in charge of the U-boat fleet investigated. Most of the crew were subtly reassigned to other ships and a new crew was assembled. But rumors were flying.

To make things worse, the admiral had a Lutheran minister come in to perform an exorcism!

While few members of the crew knew Richter, and therefore could not claim that they saw his ghost, several of them saw an officer go into the torpedo room but never come out again.

Then, in May, while the ship was cruising up and down the Channel and off the coast of Spain, the leading gunner went berserk, shrieking that he'd just seen the ghost. He jumped overboard. His body was never recovered.

Next, a petty officer jumped overboard and swam out of sight. He too was never seen again.

The ship returned to Bruges, and this time the entire crew was replaced.

On the morning of July 10, 1918, an American submarine spotted U-boat 65, wallowing seemingly out of control. Just as the captain was about to give the order to fire, the ship went up in flames and began sinking. The Americans were startled to see a German officer at the bow, standing with his arms folded. As the submarine sank, he didn't move, but just stared at the periscope of the American submarine.

There were no remains on which to hold an inquest.

The German Naval High Command didn't have any word on what had happened to the ship. On July 31st, it simply issued a statement that the U-65 was overdue and must be presumed lost with 34 officers and men.

The Killer Lake

Lake Fundudzi, in the African Transvaal, is said to be sacred to the spirit of the python that lives in it. No one bathes or fishes in the lake, though it is large and fed by many small rivers. Some say it is poisonous because it has no fish or other marine life, but crocodiles thrive in it. Stranger still, no one has ever taken any specimens of the black, muddy water so that it can be scientifically analyzed.

Dr. Harry Burnside had heard about the lake. He knew that human sacrifices had once been made there, and perhaps some still were, secretly. And he had heard that there was a death curse on any white man who disturbed the peace of the lake.

He had heard the story about the Van Blerk brothers, too. They didn't believe in curses or taboos. Jacobus van Blerk had watched his brother, Hendrik, put a six-foot collapsible canoe into the lake and paddle out on the still water. Suddenly the canoe stopped moving, although Hendrik was still paddling furiously. Then it abruptly disappeared under the water, as though a force reached up and pulled it down to the bottom. That was in 1947. Twenty-seven-year-old Hendrik van Blerk and his canoe were never seen again.

But Harry Burnside believed only in science. And for the sake of science, he determined to go to the lake in 1953 and bring back some water for examination. He took with him six bottles of several different types, with several different types of stoppers. At least one of them, he thought, would get through. He also brought along his assistant, 22-year-old William Thacker. They couldn't persuade any natives to go with them. So, they set out alone.

They parked their car seven miles from the lake and went the rest of the way on foot. They had no choice. Sometimes they had to cut through heavy brush to get to the lake.

They arrived after nightfall, so they camped close by. At dawn, they saw that the water had receded five feet from where it had been the night before. It was inky and still. But now the level was rising.

Burnside put his finger in the water and brought a drop to his mouth. Bitter, it stung his tongue.

The men filled their bottles and closed them, and then investigated the plants growing around the lake. They had never seen anything like some of them before, so they collected a few specimens to take back with them.

In the late afternoon, they started back to the car, but by nightfall, they had only gotten halfway. They camped out, agreeing to take turns staying awake to guard against wild animals. During the night, Thacker heard a popping sound and woke Burnside, but they couldn't find any reason for it. They checked the bottles, which were fine.

At dawn, they checked the bottles again before packing up. *Every one of them was empty.* One, that had a slip-on top, had burst. The others were still closed, but nothing was in them. The water could not possibly have leaked out.

They returned to the lake and refilled the bottles. Burnside was not feeling well.

They returned to the car in the afternoon and checked the bottles again. They were all right. They drove back to the local town from which they had started. When they arrived, they re-checked the bottles. They were still full.

Both Burnside and Thacker were disturbed about the Fundudzi trip, but managed to get some sleep that night. Then, in the morning, they checked the bottles again. Not a drop of the murky black water was left. None of the bottles had been opened.

Burnside now had severe stomach pains. Nine days later, he had to be taken to the hospital. As soon as he possibly could, Thacker took the plants to an expert to have them classified. The expert told him that the specimens were too old. Thacker couldn't believe it! In spite of all his efforts to keep them fresh, the plants had deteriorated to the point where they looked as if they were at least 50 years old.

Burnside went into a delirium that lasted ten hours. He died the next day. The doctors said it was enteritis, inflammation of the intestines. Could it have been from touching a drop of the inky black water to his tongue? Could it have been that poisonous? Or was something deadlier at work?

Seven months later, Thacker was out sailing when he was thrown into the water and drowned.

Coincidence? Some people said so. But the natives knew better. Lake Fundudzi had taken another victim.

3. ODD HAUNTINGS

- An astronomical observatory, haunted by its founder.

- A room that screams—

- A quilt that is pulled away in the night by invisible hands.

- A cabin cruiser that is guided to safety by a dead man.

- A brakeman who haunts the section of track where he died.

The Green Ghost of Seagrave Observatory

Seagrave Observatory in Rhode Island is a two-story building with stairs that lead up to a door in the dome. It was the home of the Skyscrapers Club for many years, a group of enthusiastic amateur astronomers. Many of them used to travel to Seagrave and camp out there during the 1960s and '70s.

There were rumors about the place being haunted.

First of all, it was set off in a forest of dark pine trees that were filled with bats.

Second, the horror story writer H. P. Lovecraft used to attend Skyscrapers meetings in the 1930s, so Seagrave had a history and tradition of mystery.

Third, Frank Seagrave, who built the observatory for his own personal use in the 1870s, was concerned with his privacy. He allowed no one to use the telescope except for his assistant, and of course himself.

So it wasn't to his ghost's liking, it was said, to have all those noisy astronomy students wandering around.

While using the telescope, club members reported hearing loud footsteps in an alcove or the basement of the building. When they were investigated, the footsteps could not be explained away.

Sometimes there were footsteps on the stairs leading up to the dome, but while the sounds came all the way up to the door, no one would come in.

Soon, the students began leaving the door to the dome unlocked so that they could get out fast if it became necessary.

Some members slept in the observatory. They stayed in the little alcove on the ground floor, leaving the outside door partly open. Others slept in a clubhouse across the wide lawn opposite the observatory.

One night, a member of the Skyscrapers Club, who was staying in the clubhouse, looked across the lawn at the observatory. He saw a glowing green ball of light—or gas—hovering over the sleeping students. He had never seen anything like it, but whatever it was, it didn't look friendly! He gave a bloodcurdling scream, waking everybody on both sides of the lawn. The green ghost vanished as half a dozen club members ran out the door in their underwear.

The ghost appeared again many times over the next few years, and it was seen—or heard—by many people. Some said it would vaporize further and disappear in front of Frank Seagrave's portrait.

Eventually, meetings of the Skyscrapers Club were moved to another location. Seagrave's Observatory was "too cold," they said. At last Frank Seagrave was able to get some rest!

The Screaming Room

It was a small house in a poor neighborhood in Sussex, England—nothing fancy—and not very old. But what happened there was macabre.

The year was 1947. World War II was over and it was hard to find a place to live. Helen and her brother, Hank, had just been discharged from the army, and they were delighted to find the little house, even if it was less than half furnished. They were both used to roughing it, and it was really great to have a whole house to themselves. They each invited a friend to visit for a couple of weeks.

Helen took the best room—the one on the second floor. It was the largest and had a real bed in it, not just an army cot. She settled down to sleep with an ecstatic sense of comfort. It was the middle of the night when she woke up. The room was dark—not unusual, she thought—but did it seem darker than normal? And there was a heaviness, a stillness. She had a strong feeling that something was in there with her.

"You're being ridiculous," she told herself. "You're just not used to having a room to yourself."

But she couldn't get back to sleep. She began to sweat, to see shapes in the blackness, and a cold terror crept over her. She forced herself to reach out and switch on the light. The room was ugly—but no one was in there with her—no one she could see.

The same thing happened the next night. Helen was beginning to dread going upstairs.

Then the third night, she woke with a sudden shock and sat straight up in bed. The room was vibrating with sound, as if a scream had just ended and was reverberating through the air. Was the room screaming? Or was it her own scream? Or did it come from downstairs?

Helen leaped out of bed and rushed down the stairs. As she did, she heard a strange clicking sound. But Hank and their friends were all sound asleep.

The next day, Helen suggested that it would be easier for her to start breakfast in the morning and lock up at night if she slept downstairs.

"What? Give up the best room?" Hank said. "Well, none of that noble self-sacrifice for me. I'm moving upstairs into that room before you change your mind."

Hank lasted three days in the upstairs room. Then he said—not looking Helen in the eye—it was really only right for their guest to have the "best room." So he moved out and his friend, William, moved upstairs.

The next morning when William came down to breakfast, both Hank and Helen looked at him closely. He seemed tired, but said he had slept well, and he got quite irritated with their questions.

William's temperament did not improve as the days passed. He grew more and more distant, red-eyed and silent, and spent increasing amounts of time in the room. Then, when he had been visiting the house for exactly two weeks, he started screaming—just letting out one ghastly, bloodcurdling scream after another.

Neighbors called the police, but they couldn't quiet him. At last a doctor put him under sedation and he was taken away by ambulance to a mental hospital, where he spent the next year.

Jennifer, Helen's friend, was so shaken that Helen had to spend the next couple of weeks taking care of her. A few months later, Jennifer attempted suicide, and she too was taken to a mental hospital.

Hank and Helen finally talked about the room. Why hadn't they discussed it before? They admitted that they thought they'd be laughed at. They had both heard the screaming, and Hank claimed he had felt the presence of some kind of horrible "cat thing."

Helen at last got thoroughly sick herself, so, it wasn't until some months later that she talked with one of the neighbors about the house. It had originally been built as a bungalow by a small commercial builder who added the upstairs room later. He divided the house in half, renting out the right-hand part to an old woman and her daughter and living in the left-hand part himself. He soon moved on, but the daughter of the old woman had become obsessed with spiritualism and used to experiment with an Ouija board. What ghastly, inhuman thing had she unleashed?

"Where can I find her?" Helen asked.

"Won't do you any good to find that one," said her neighbor. "They carted her off to the madhouse, they did, just a few weeks before you and your brother moved in."

The Christmas Quilt

In 1957, the day before her daughter Florence came to visit, Mrs. Monroe pulled out the old box containing the patchwork quilt. She had found it in the top of a closet when she and her husband had bought the Poy Sippi, Wisconsin, farmhouse two years ago. It was a charming old-fashioned quilt, red and yellow and beautifully handmade, but she had never put it out on a bed before. What was she waiting for?

When Florence arrived, she admired the quilt, and went to bed that night expecting to get a good night's sleep. But that's not what happened.

At about midnight, she woke up with a start as the quilt was jerked away from her. She grabbed onto it with both hands, but the quilt kept pulling away as if someone was at the other end of it, and a woman's voice said, "Give me back my Christmas quilt."

Florence was petrified. There was no one there, but the tugging didn't stop and neither did the voice. Florence held on to the quilt all night. It wasn't until dawn that the tugging stopped.

That was the beginning. Soon everyone wanted to test out the quilt.

The first one was Mrs. Monroe's other daughter, Margaret, who brought her own daughter with her. They gave up on the quilt shortly after midnight when it got painfully hot.

Margaret's 18-year-old son was next. He was sleeping on a couch and got his cousin Richard to watch from a roll-away bed they had set up across the room. Right after midnight, Richard saw the quilt pull itself off Tom. He said that it raised up about 12 inches and floated toward the foot of the couch, landing on the floor.

Margaret's daughter had a boyfriend who gave it a try. When, at about midnight, the quilt started to move, he jumped out of bed. Then the cover straightened itself out until it was as smooth as if the bed had just been made.

A cousin from California had the quilt sent out there so that her family could try it. The quilt got very hot, she reported in a letter that she sent back with the quilt, whenever anyone tried to sleep under it. They also heard footsteps, as if someone was "running around the house in his bare feet."

Finally, Mr. Monroe put the quilt on his own bed. At first, when he felt the tugging, he hung on to it. Then, he thought, why not let go and see what happens?

"The crazy thing dragged itself across the floor,"

he said, "and curled up under the dresser."

The Christmas quilt, after being sent here and there and "tried" by person after person, finally got the last laugh.

On Halloween, in 1963, the *Oshkosh Northwestern* sponsored a ghosthunting event, in which two women would sleep under the quilt while three other women stood guard.

The Christmas quilt did absolutely *nothing*.

In the end, the ghost or the poltergeist or the entity that so loved the Christmas quilt got its way. None of the family members wanted it on the bed. So the Christmas quilt was put out strictly for show—and given a wide berth.

Lost at Sea

Mike was a sport fisherman, in the market for a new boat. A friend gave him the name of a woman with a boat she was trying to unload. He told Mike that she was desperate, and he could get a good deal.

Mike went with the woman to a marina in Sheepshead Bay, where he got a look at the boat. It was beautiful—a cabin cruiser, fully equipped and in perfect shape—a boat to dream about.

"I want to get rid of it—just make me an offer," said the woman. That's how Mike picked up a $50,000 boat for $10,000.

After they signed the papers, the woman relaxed and began to talk. The boat had belonged to her husband, Wayne, and he had taken great care of it. When they found it deserted, they knew Wayne had to be lost at sea. Nothing else could have gotten him away from the boat. But his body had never been found.

Mike moved the boat to his own dock in Coney Island. He took it out a couple of times and soon he was sailing it like an old pro.

It was late in the afternoon on a hot, sticky day in August when Mike, his cousin Alan, and another friend, Peter, went fishing. It wasn't a good day to go out—the sea was rough and fog was rolling in. Soon they had gone so far that they couldn't see the shore.

Mike turned off the engine and they sat there fishing, drinking beer. It got dark. They were telling stories, and the fog got thicker. Soon it was pitch-black all around them. And strangely quiet. They couldn't even hear the buoy bells.

About ten o'clock they figured they'd go back. Mike went to turn on the engine, but it wouldn't start. Then they tried to use the radio. It was jammed.

As they sat on the deck, trying to figure out what to do next, the cabin and deck lights went out. They were in what seemed like complete darkness.

They started blaming each other, fighting. Then Mike mentioned that the boat's previous owner had been lost at sea.

"Maybe it's that guy Wayne's fault," Mike said. "He probably doesn't want anyone else sailing his boat."

"No," said Alan, "no, he's a good guy—look at what good care he took of it."

Finally, sometime after midnight, they decided to go to sleep in the cabin and just wait for daylight.

The next thing Mike knew, it was morning. He was the first up, feeling hung over, headache-y. Then he heard it—car traffic! He stumbled out onto the deck. They were back in a marina. Traffic was going by on the parkway.

Then he saw that the boat was actually tied up at the dock. Somebody had brought them in—through all that fog—and tied up the boat.

He woke Alan and Peter. They were as surprised as he was. The three of them tried to find someone who had seen the boat coming in, but no one could tell them anything.

The strangest part of it was that they weren't at Mike's dock. They were in Sheepshead Bay, where Mike had seen the boat for the first time. Only one person could have brought them there—and that person had been lost at sea.

Ghost of the Brakeman

Vic was visiting his friends, Charley and his wife, Janet, in Clinton, Ohio. Late one night they decided to go out to the now abandoned Erie Lackawanna railway tracks to catch a glimpse of the ghost of the brakeman, who was said to haunt a curved stretch of track between two dark woods. Charley had once seen the ghost, he said, and ever since a story appeared about it in the local paper, he had been wild to go back.

When Vic and Charley got to the area, the place was packed with people who were also waiting, sitting on car hoods, drinking beer, lounging on deck chairs, eating fried chicken. There was even a card table set up and a few people playing bridge.

"I was afraid of this," said Charley. "Ever since that story, this place has been overrun. He'll never show with this crowd."

A few nights later it was raining really hard. Janet was cutting up a homemade berry pie for a late snack when Charley jumped up.

"Tonight's the night!" he said. "Let's go!"

As they drove the dark, rainslicked roads to the tracks, Charley told the story of the brakeman's ghost.

It was a rainy night when it happened. The young brakeman was working the graveyard shift for the Erie Lackawanna. It was during the 1930s when a man, if he was lucky enough to have a job, worked long hours. The brakeman had to sit outdoors all night and signal the trains to guide them along the hazardous stretch of track between the dark woods. He carried a large, yellow lantern that he swung back and forth.

The brakeman's job was an important one, especially on rainy nights like this one. It was cold and lonely. The brakeman always kept a bottle of whiskey beside him for warmth and company.

One particular rainy night, perhaps with a little too much drink in him, the brakeman stumbled as he crossed the tracks and dropped his lantern. Maybe he twisted his ankle or did some other damage to his legs. But he couldn't get up. He did manage to pull himself partially off the tracks, but not altogether. The train passed over him, cutting off both his legs. It must have been an agonizing death. They found him the next day in a huge pool of blood.

Vic, Charley and Janet waited beside the tracks, standing in what was now a light summer rain. The place was deserted.

Then, suddenly, they saw it—a sort of red spot—coming down the tracks. Dim at first, it moved back and forth like a pendulum.

"That can't be it," Janet said. "A brakeman's light would be yellow."

The hair on the back of Vic's neck stood up.

Charley was crazy with excitement. "Come on," he said. "We've got to get closer!"

They started walking down the tracks towards the red spot. The only sounds were the crunch of gravel under their feet and Janet screeching after them to get down and come back.

As the spot came closer, Vic could see that it was just a glow, really—a ball of red light about the size of a saucer, about the size of a lantern light without the lantern.

But that wasn't the strangest part. It was the way the light moved. It swung sort of awkwardly back and forth, hobbling about three feet from the ground—just the way a blood-soaked lantern would if it were carried by a legless brakeman!

They got to within 15 feet of the light—all the while ready to turn on their heels and run.

Vic couldn't believe what he was seeing. "Maybe it's some kind of swamp gas—or static electricity in the air from the lightning," he whispered to Charley.

Suddenly the light blinked out. Janet, way behind them, started shrieking and pointing. They turned and looked. The light had blinked on again *on the other side of them*—and it went on swinging and bobbling eerily down the tracks.

"Did you see *that?*" yelled Charley. "It knows we're here!"

Without saying another word to each other, they jumped off the tracks and raced to the car. Charley grabbed Janet and pushed her inside. He threw the car in gear just as the light disappeared into the far woods and blinked through the trees.

Driving home, they were all quiet until Janet spoke. "Where do you think he's going?" she asked.

"No telling," said Charley. "These tracks go on for miles. He could be going anywhere—but he always comes back."

4. ANIMALS OF DOOM

- Encounters with a friendly dog bring death.

- Hordes of mice scurry away from a New York brownstone—exactly like rats deserting a sinking ship.

- A great white bird appears whenever an Oxenham is about to die.

The Black Dog of Hanging Hills

Many legends have been told of frightening black dogs that haunt deserted roads, gloomy castles, even town houses. But the black dog of Hanging Hills is gentle and friendly, a splendid companion with whom to spend an afternoon—and he is deadlier than all the rest. If you ever meet him, you'll know him by two peculiar features: One, he leaves no footprints. Two, he seems to bark occasionally, but never makes a sound.

When you see him the first time, he brings you joy. He follows you wherever you go, wags his tail, waits for you if you stop along the way.

The second time you meet him is a time of sorrow for you.

But, if you see him twice, don't go back to Hanging Hills. Because the third time you see the black dog, you die.

W.H.C. Pynchon told part of the story almost a century ago. A geologist, he was visiting Meriden, Connecticut, because he wanted to see some unusual rock formations he had heard about. When he first saw the black dog, it was standing on a high boulder and looking down at him, wagging its tail. When Pynchon continued on his way, the dog ran alongside. When the geologist stopped at an inn for lunch, the dog waited outside for him. They spent the afternoon together, and it wasn't until dusk that the dog took off into the woods.

Pynchon didn't go back to Hanging Hills for a number of years. When he did it was in February. He went with another geologist, who knew the area fairly well. In fact, his friend had told Pynchon that he had seen the peculiar little dog twice before on his visits.

The next day, the two men began climbing the mountain called West Peak. They chose to squeeze through a gap between two cliffs. It was a particularly dark space that turned out to be rather icy. As they neared the top of the mountain, they looked up and saw the black dog high on the rocks, wagging its tail and barking—without making a sound.

Delighted to see him, they continued their ascent, looking forward to greeting the dog when they got to the top.

Then, unbelievably, Pynchon's friend lost his footing on the ice, and before Pynchon could come to his rescue, smashed down the cliff, crashing violently against the rocks below. It was the third time Pynchon's friend had seen the dog. And the second time for Pynchon, who experienced great sorrow at the loss of his friend.

Later, Pynchon was told the story of the black dog

by local people, and he wrote about his experience after that. In view of this knowledge, it is difficult to understand why he went back to West Peak to retrace the steps he had taken with his friend.

But perhaps you've already figured out what happened.

Pynchon's broken body was found in approximately the same spot that his friend's body had been found a couple of years before.

Did he see the black dog? We'll never know for sure. But others have since reported seeing the dog. Pynchon was not the last climber to die on West Peak. The most recent victim died there in 1972 on Thanksgiving Day. How many times do you think the climber had been there before?

The Psychic Mice

Actor Raymond Massey and his wife, Dorothy, were tired of staying at hotels whenever they had to be in New York, and they decided to find a small house where they could stay and would eventually call home.

Dorothy did the house-hunting and she came up with two brownstone houses that she liked. First, she took Ray to see her favorite, but from the moment he walked into it, he disliked it intensely. It felt cold, he said, like a tomb.

The other house was right across the street. He agreed with Dorothy on that one and they bought it.

One day, after they had settled in, Dorothy was out walking the dog, when she met a woman who turned out to be her new neighbor from across the street.

"I liked your house so much," Dorothy told her, "I thought it was much nicer than ours, but Ray didn't like it."

"It's a nice house," said her neighbor, "but we've got such a problem with mice. I've tried everything but can't get rid of them."

A short time after that, Dorothy was looking out the window, and couldn't believe her eyes. There were waves of mice, coming out of the basement of the house across the street. They were disoriented, running, stumbling, scurrying along the street. Dorothy had heard of rats leaving a sinking ship, but she found it hard to believe that mice would choose to leave a perfectly good brownstone.

A few days later, Ray called her attention to a front-page story about a socialite who had committed suicide.

"That must be the woman who lives across the street," Dorothy said. "Check the address." It was the woman who owned the house with the mice—without the mice, now.

The next occupant turned out to be a beautiful blonde, who had been set up there by a wealthy playboy. Just before his death made front-page news, another generation of mice moved out of the house.

Dorothy began watching the house across the street with a kind of horror. It stayed vacant for quite a while. Finally, it was purchased by an "important" businessman, and she stopped paying attention.

One day when she was watering some plants in the window box, she saw the mice again—going through the same routine. What was going to happen now?

She didn't have to wait long to find out. It was on the front page of *The Times* again. A prominent businessman who flew his own plane was coming home from a trip to Canada, when he cracked up over the Hudson. He drowned before rescuers could reach him.

They recognized the address—it was the house across the street!

Then a strange thing happened. The Masseys had had mice in the house themselves ever since the first exodus of mice from across the street. Nothing seemed to get rid of them—even cats. But suddenly their own mice began to leave. Can you imagine what went on in their heads?

No, nothing terrible happened to Dorothy or Ray. But the mice were smart to leave. Because, shortly afterwards, the Masseys' furnace blew up.

The White Bird of Death

Whenever a member of the Oxenham family dies, a white bird is seen—usually in the bedroom or trying to enter the bedroom, of the dying person. Sometimes the birds are seen in other places as well. This has been going on for almost 400 years. A close family member generally sees the bird. Sometimes, doctors and nurses and ministers see it, or hear it. But it always makes an appearance.

One of the most famous instances was the death of Margaret Oxenham. She had been unable to decide which of two men she should marry. Finally, she made up her mind and, on her wedding day, a huge feast was held at the manor. The bride's father was having a grand time, until he saw a white bird fluttering around his daughter's head. No one else seemed to notice it—or hear it—least of all Margaret. The next day was the wedding. Evidently, Margaret had made the right decision about which man to marry—but the wrong one for her safety. Because the rejected suitor leaped out of the crowd, either stabbed or shot her (there are two stories), and then killed himself.

A more recent occurrence deals with the death of Mrs. John Oxenham in 1975. The woman's daughter, who lived in London, was making a trip to Cornwall to see her sick mother, but she had no idea the illness was life-threatening. So, she stopped off to visit a friend along the way. During her visit, a large white bird stayed around outside the house, perching on the windowsill and the roof. No one said very much about it at first, but after it was seen by many people for several days, they began to talk about it. No one had seen a bird like that in the area before.

"Oh, no—could that be *the* white bird?" Mrs. Oxenham's daughter had never connected this white bird with the legend. Did that mean, she wondered, that *she* was going to die?

Frightened, she packed quickly and left for Cornwall. The bird left when she did. A week later, Mrs. John Oxenham was dead.

5.
POLTERGEIST!

- A dish-throwing spirit successfully disrupts a young woman's social life—until it meets a voodoo priest.

- A mischievous poltergeist plays clever games with costumes and props in the theatre.

- Old Jeffrey does everything a poltergeist is supposed to do, but he can't get any respect.

The Case of the Possessive Poltergeist

Do poltergeists have emotions—the way people do? Can they become so jealous of the people they haunt that they don't want them to go out or have any friends? That seems to be what happened in the case of the dish-throwing poltergeist of Nelly Roca.

It took place in the bayou country near New Orleans in 1963. Nelly Roca had just moved into a mobile home. She was about to serve dinner one night to a couple of her friends when plates began to leap out of the cupboard. One by one they hurled themselves—or rather, were hurled by something—across the room. Every plate Nelly owned was shattered.

It took a few days before she was willing to go back inside the mobile home. She brought a friend and more plates and they made some coffee. Then, at exactly eight o'clock, the cups and saucers started dancing around on the table—until one by one—they crashed down on the floor. Nelly's friend beat a hasty retreat.

A few days later, Nelly was asked to leave the mobile home. Rumors were going around, she was told, and if word were to get around about the ghost, it wouldn't be good publicity for the trailer park.

About a month later, Nelly had settled in a small apartment and was in the living room talking with some friends. They heard sounds from the kitchen— you guessed it—dishes were jumping off the shelves and then, one by one, getting thrown *by something* against the walls and smashing on the floor.

It was getting clear that the ghost—or poltergeist or whatever it was—was not going to tolerate her having guests. But Nelly had no intention of isolating herself. She bought a set of plastic dishes, and that seemed to solve the problem for a while.

Then, on the 5th of April, 1964, Nelly went to a friend's house to visit. The poltergeist evidently went also. No sooner had she walked in when the dishes on the kitchen table began to shake and the plates on the shelves began to smash against the walls. Nelly's friend said, "Nelly, for pity's sake, get out of here!" and Nelly rushed away. As soon as she left, the dishes stopped moving.

Obviously, Nelly was no longer being asked out very much. Finally, in January 1965, she was invited to a small housewarming. And it happened again—plates, cups and saucers, bowls—they all began flying around the kitchen. Nelly didn't have to be asked to leave. She sped off at once and the destruction stopped.

It kept on happening. Every time Nelly Roca went out—or had any company—dishes went berserk.

Finally, in August, she and a few of the friends she had left went to consult Henry Citron, a voodoo priest, who lived deep in the bayou country. He sat her in a shack together with him and his disciples, who carried torches and strangely marked boxes. One of the boxes contained plates and bowls, which were put on small tables around Nelly.

As usual, the plates and bowls began to shake and get thrown onto the floor. The priest and his disciples started chanting and formed a circle around Nelly. One of them lifted a second box, and held it up with the lid open. A couple of plates were thrown at the box, but both missed. Then one plate rose, as if someone were picking it up and attempting to place it in the box. The priest shook a gourd and lunged towards the box. Quickly, the disciples slammed the lid shut and nailed it closed.

That was the end of it. The poltergeist was trapped in the box. Nelly Roca never had any more trouble from it.

A Poltergeist Goes to the Theatre

When you think of the number of things that can go wrong backstage without the help of a poltergeist, it's mind-boggling to imagine what might happen if one really went to work. (A few probably have.)

Beatrice Lillie, the famous British comedienne, claimed she had a personal poltergeist that followed her around. It didn't make any real trouble, though, until she was at the Palm Beach Playhouse, starring in "An Evening with Beatrice Lillie."

First, one of the actresses in the show, Constance Carpenter, had a quick change to make. Since her dressing room was not near the stage, Miss Lillie agreed to let her keep the costume in her own dressing room.

At one performance, when Constance Carpenter tried to get into her costume, she couldn't! The hem was basted together with big stitches all the way across! The actress ripped out the stitches and raced onto the stage—just a little late for her cue.

They tried to find out who did it, without success. The only people who had keys to the dressing room were Bea Lillie herself and her dresser, a girl from a local Florida family.

After that, Constance Carpenter kept her costume in her own dressing room.

The second time the poltergeist got out of control was with a black fan that Bea Lillie used in the second part of the show. She had left it on her dressing table when she went out to do the previous number. Her dresser had gone with her, locking the door behind them. When Miss Lillie got back to the dressing room and reached for the fan, it was gone. The two women looked everywhere they could think of, but couldn't find it. Miss Lillie finally went on stage with a different fan that she dug out of her wardrobe trunk.

Then, two days later, the fan was back on the dressing table—right where it had been left.

The third incident had to do with a great Japanese headdress—an elaborate black wig with many tiny decorative sticks securely fastened in it. Before one performance, the sticks were removed—every one of them—and set neatly beside the wig on the dressing table.

None of this really annoyed Bea Lillie, until the poltergeist made off with one of her rings. She looked all over for it. Then, suddenly, even though she *knew* it couldn't possibly be there, she was drawn to climb up on a chair and look on the high shelf in her closet. Sure enough, there it was!

The poltergeist had been at work before that (and since) in Bea Lillie's New York apartment, but, fortunately, it never again went to the theatre.

A Poltergeist Named Jeffrey

If ever a poltergeist tried for classy credentials, it was Jeffrey, the entity who chose to haunt the Wesley house. The head of that family was Reverend Samuel Wesley, father of 19 children, including John, who went on to found the Methodist Church. Jeffrey was really in over his head.

It started on December 2, 1716, with knocks on the door and groans, but when the doors were opened, no one was there.

First it was only the servants who heard the knockings, and the strange noises in the house. But very soon the children were hearing them too, and telling their mother about them. Her reaction—"I'll believe it when I hear it"—was short-lived, because she was called to the nursery, where she heard for herself a cradle rocking when no cradle was in the room.

No one had told Mr. Wesley anything about this, so far. When he did hear about it, he said it was utter rubbish and that some of the children or the servants were playing games. He even took to spying on the girls from time to time to see if he could detect any deception.

Finally he heard the sounds himself during family prayers. Evidently, the poltergeist didn't much approve of King George, because it knocked continuously when prayers for him were being said. The spirit even tried to push the Reverend around—and got away with it a few times. Wesley countered by buying a mastiff, a huge animal that he thought would be a good watchdog.

There were so many noises now and other manifestations, too—including odd animals rushing about, thunderous sounds on the stairs, and an old man wandering around in a nightgown—that the Wesley family had gotten quite used to being haunted. They dubbed the poltergeist "Jeffrey," and found him very boring, making so much noise that they couldn't hear each other, or doing annoying things like opening doors and fiddling with latches.

"Oh, don't pay any attention—it's just old Jeffrey," the girls would say.

Sometimes, for fun, they'd chase the sounds from room to room. Or tease him by saying that they thought the noises were being made by rats, or some other natural cause. The knockings got very loud when they did that.

Eventually, the only one in the house who was frightened of Jeffrey was the mastiff, who would grovel in fear and creep away before the noises began.

The Reverend was advised to leave the house. But he refused to "fly from the devil," and kept a diary that recorded every run-in he had with the creature.

Jeffrey did not stay long at the Wesley home. He was gone by the end of January. He probably got sick of being treated with such disrespect.

6. A MATTER OF TIME

7 DECEMBER 1941

- A fateful day in the life of a North American Indian tribe—replayed 100 years later.

- A message from the future that appears on the sidewalk of an Indiana town.

- A bullet that takes 20 years to complete its deadly work.

Massacre of the Cree

The storm had come up fast—and there had been no warning. If Denny had thought he'd have to deal with the torrential rains that he was fighting now, he never would have come out for this "relaxing" day of fishing and hunting.

The weather had looked perfect when he started out with an Indian guide, a packhorse, and a collapsible boat, in which he had decided to return while the Indian and the packhorse took the overland route. The day's sport had turned out to be great, but the boat was undoubtedly a mistake.

One of the original officers of the Northwest Mounted Police, Cecil A. Denny was stationed at Fort Walsh on the Oldman River in the part of the Northwest Territories that is now the Province of Alberta in Canada. He knew that sudden wild storms like this were not uncommon.

Now he practically lost the oars as the boat crashed against a particularly large stone. The frail boat was definitely not meant to function in these swirling rapids and whirlpools. It was getting battered and snagged on the rocky, shallow riverbed. It was only a matter of time before it would be completely destroyed.

On the left side of the river, he thought he could see a clump of trees through the relentless rain. Anything would be better than this.

He managed to get the boat to the bank of the river and dragged it up on the shore. As he ran ahead to get some shelter under the trees, he heard Indian drums rising above the thunder, and chanting.

He moved through the trees, which unloaded another shower of water on him, and peered beyond them.

He saw a clearing in which there was an Indian camp. Beyond that some shaggy horses were grazing.

The peculiar thing was that neither the horses nor the people seemed to be paying any attention to the horrendous weather that was going on all around. The little children were playing out in the open as if no rain were coming down. The flaps to the teepees were open—and most of the Indians Denny knew feared thunder and usually drew the flaps of their tents closed at the first sign of a storm.

But that was all right, he thought. They were Crees—he could tell from the decorations on the teepees—and the police had a good relationship with the Crees. He could probably get some food and maybe a chance to get dry.

That was when the lightning hit him, and he found

himself flat on the ground, enveloped in a strange blue flame.

He lay unconscious for a few minutes, and then managed to get up and start for the camp. But it wasn't there. The tents, the people, the playing children, the horses—they were all gone.

He climbed a hill, expecting that from there he could see them travelling off—but there was no sign of them. Maybe he'd been unconscious for longer than he thought?

Denny knew that it made no sense to try to get back to the fort by boat, so he began walking. He made it back—mostly by guesswork—by around midnight.

A couple of days passed, and as soon as he could get away, he went back to pick up the boat that he'd abandoned along the upper reaches of the Oldman River. The Indian guide and the packhorse went with him.

When they finally found the boat, Denny and his guide carefully went over the ground where he had seen the Indians. There was no evidence that they had been there—only a few rings of stones, overgrown by grass, some bleached bones, and a couple of human skulls.

As they travelled back, the Indian guide told Denny that his grandfather had often talked about a terrible massacre of Cree Indians that had taken place at that very spot. The killers were a murderous bunch of Blackfeet, the Crees' traditional enemies.

It was a sneak attack, in which the Blackfeet killed every man, woman, and child, torched the teepees, and stole everything else. That had happened when his grandfather was a little boy.

Denny suddenly realized what he had seen. It was a reenactment of the day of the massacre. If he hadn't been struck by lightning, perhaps he might have witnessed the whole thing. That would explain why the people didn't notice the weather—because they were experiencing the weather at another place in time. He had heard of such ghostly reenactments of battles—in England, usually—when some kind of great or terrible event took place. But if it happened in England, it probably happened in other places as well.

How many times, he wondered—in the generations since the massacre—had the cruel, barbaric attack been replayed? How many times would it act itself out again in the future?

Off the Time Track?

It was the morning of December 7th in Owensville, Indiana. Painted in huge letters on the pavement outside the elementary school were the words:

REMEMBER PEARL HARBOR

Not so surprising, you say? Well, it was on December 7, 1941, that the attack on Pearl Harbor took place. But the year that the message appeared on the sidewalk in Indiana was 1939—two years before!

The Bullet That Waited

It was a miracle, they said, that he had lived. In those days, during World War I, if a bullet were to lodge in the heart, it was always fatal. There was no way they could operate without killing him. And in fact, they couldn't understand how he could possibly be alive anyway. So the doctors sent John Russell Makinson home, expecting that he wouldn't live very long.

John did very well. The bullet in his heart gave him no trouble at all. He worked—operating a small hotel—and played and married and lived a perfectly normal life.

Then 20 years after the battle in which he had been shot, he and his wife took a pleasure trip abroad, which included a stopover at Gallipoli in Turkey. He wanted to revisit the spot at which he'd been shot.

The area was large and they walked for some time before John saw it—the narrow path that led to the ravine into which he had fallen when he was hit.

"That's it," he told her excitedly, "that's where the blighters got me!"

Then, to his wife's horror, he stumbled and fell to the ground. He was dead. The autopsy showed that the bullet imbedded in his heart had shifted position, completing the fateful job that it had started 20 years before.

7. DARK DREAMS

- A voice from the grave comes direct from the coffin.

- A ghost haunts a Scottish castle, but the ghost is alive.

- A horrifying dream of violent death is shared by friends.

- Mark Twain foresees the death of his younger brother in a true dream.

- Lincoln has two dreams of death— and talks about them—just before he is assassinated.

Dream of a Cold Ghost

The day of Anthony's grandfather's funeral was bitingly cold. No one wanted to stand around outside. And, anyway, at Catholic funerals, the mourners don't generally wait to see the casket put into the ground. It just hangs on a kind of gurney or trestle over the open grave. There are flowers all around, so you can't see the machinery. Then, when everybody leaves, the gravediggers come back and lower the casket into the hole.

On this particular day in February, Mass was said, and everyone hurried to their cars. The gravediggers would do the rest.

That night Anthony had a weird dream. First he heard a cracking sound, like a rusty spring.

Then came his grandfather's voice. "Tony, Tony, I'm really cold. Tell them to put me down—please tell them to put me down."

Then came the cracking noise again.

When Anthony woke up in the morning, he told his mother about the dream.

"Forget it," she said, "it's nothing."

Anthony had the same dream the next night.

It wasn't until he visited the grave a few days later that Anthony found out what happened.

It had been so cold the day of the funeral that the gravediggers couldn't dig the hole. They had to leave the casket unburied, just hanging from the machine. They left it that way for two nights.

The Ghost of Ballaculish

Could dreams have a very different purpose—and reality—from anything we've ever imagined? Take the startling case of the Boultons—an English couple who arranged to rent Ballaculish, a stately home in Scotland, for the summer.

Mr. Boulton was a student of Scottish folklore, and Mrs. Boulton was attracted to Scotland as well. For many years, she had had a recurring dream in which she lived in a magnificent house in the Highlands. Everyone who knew her knew about her "dream house"— how she knew every inch of it—every staircase, every room, every piece of furniture—even though she had never set eyes on it in a waking state. Sooner or later, she was convinced, as she travelled around in Scotland, she would discover her dream house.

Jokingly, Mr. Boulton had asked Lady Beresford, the owner of Ballaculish, whether it had any ghosts. She had written him that there was just one that she knew of—an extremely amiable woman whom she often saw walking through the rooms looking at everything as if she were inspecting the premises.

Finally the day came when the Boultons were due to move in. Lady Beresford waited for them to arrive so that she could say hello and turn over the keys personally.

Her tenants greeted her with excitement and enthusiasm.

"It's so nice that you waited to show us round," smiled Mrs. Boulton, "but you didn't need to. I know this house as I know my own name!"

It was the house Mrs. Boulton had seen in her dreams! She proceeded to escort her landlady and her husband through the maze of corridors and rooms, commenting on a change here and there—even becoming confused because a staircase was missing (it had been walled off). Mrs. Boulton was thrilled and incredulous—but no more so than her landlady, who never spoke a word.

Because Lady Beresford had seen her new tenant before. She was the "amiable woman" who had so often "inspected the premises"—the ghost of Ballaculish.

Dream of Disaster

Henry Armitt Brown was a lawyer and lecturer—not the kind of person you'd expect to have a strange psychic encounter. But the dream he had—and the experiences that followed—are not at all what anyone would expect.

It happened in November 1865, when he was a law student in New York. It was a cold, blustery evening. Henry was in bed before midnight and asleep shortly after. He had hardly lost consciousness when he seemed to hear loud and confused noises and felt a choking sensation at his throat, as if it were being grasped by a strong hand.

He woke up (in the dream) and found himself lying on his back on the cobblestones of a narrow street, struggling beneath the body of a heavy man with long, uncombed hair and a grizzly beard. The man had one hand at Henry's throat and the other was holding his wrists.

Henry realized he was about to be killed, and he fought back furiously. They rolled over on the stones and then he saw the man pick up a shiny—evidently brand new— hatchet. Henry made one last intense effort to get free of his attacker, and, as he did, he saw over the man's shoulder that some of his friends were rushing to his rescue. His closest friend was ahead of the rest and he leaped onto the back of the thug. The hatchet flashed, and Henry felt a dull blow on his forehead. He fell back onto the ground as a numbness spread from his head to his body. A warm liquid flowed down on his face and into his mouth, and he realized it was blood.

Then he seemed to be suspended in the air a few feet over his body, looking at his body on the ground, the hatchet stuck in his head. He could hear the cries of his friends, loud at first and then growing fainter and fading away into silence.

A delightful sensation came over him—of relaxation and peace. He heard superb music, smelled wonderful scents and seemed to be lying on a bed of downy softness—when he woke up. He had not been asleep for more than half an hour.

Early the next morning, Henry and his best friend were walking to law school together.

"I had a weird dream about you last night," his friend told him. "I fell asleep about midnight and dreamed that I was passing through a narrow street when I heard noises and cries of murder. Then I saw you lying on your back, fighting off a roughneck who was holding you down. I ran forward, but as I got there, he hit you on the head with a hatchet and killed you instantly. Quite a vivid dream. When I woke up there were tears on my face, believe it or not."

"What was the killer like?" Henry asked.

His friend described the man precisely.

A week later, Henry was visiting another of his friends in New Jersey.

"My husband," the man's wife said, "had a horrible dream about you the other night. He dreamed that you were killed in a street fight. He ran to help you, but before he could reach you, your enemy had hit you with a big club."

"Oh, no," said her husband, coming into the room, "he killed you with a hatchet—a brand new, shiny one, too."

Henry had told no one about his dream, and Henry's two friends did not know each other.

Mark Twain's Dream

Samuel Clemens (Mark Twain) was very fond of his younger brother, Henry. One night, while visiting at his sister's house in St. Louis, he had a dream that Henry was dead and lying in a metal coffin that was supported on two chairs. On his chest lay a bouquet of white flowers with a single crimson blossom in the center.

He woke up terribly depressed, believing his dream was true—and it took several hours for him to realize that it wasn't. He told his sister about the dream and then put it out of his mind.

The brothers were both scheduled to travel down the Mississippi that week. Henry was going on the *Pennsylvania*, which was leaving St. Louis the next day. Samuel was due to follow on a different ship, the *A.T. Lacey*, two days later.

Everything was going as planned. Then, when Samuel's ship touched at one of the scheduled stops, a voice from the landing shouted that the *Pennsylvania* had blown up just below Memphis—and that 150 lives had been lost.

Samuel was horrified. At each stop along the way, new reports were issued. First it appeared that Henry had escaped injury—then that he was scalded beyond recovery—finally that he had died.

When Samuel arrived at Memphis, he went to the place where the bodies were laid out. Most of the coffins were of unpainted wood, but because Henry had been so young and handsome, the ladies of Memphis set up a fund and bought him a metal case. It was supported by two chairs.

Samuel's brother looked exactly the way he did in the dream—except there were no flowers.

As Samuel stood and watched, an elderly lady came into the room with a large white bouquet and put it on Henry's chest. In the center was a single red rose.

Lincoln's Dreams

Lincoln knew that he was going to be assassinated, and he even knew approximately when. He knew it— at least partly—from his dreams.

About a month before he was assassinated, he had one dream that was so powerful, so real, that he couldn't get it out of his mind.

He had gone to bed very late after waiting for news from the front. He fell asleep quickly and started dreaming:

He was in his room at the White House and there was a deathlike stillness about him. He heard subdued sobs, as if many people were weeping. Within his dream, he went downstairs, walking from one empty room to another, and hearing mournful sounds. Where were the people who were grieving? He kept on until he arrived at the East Room. Before him was a catafalque, a raised sort of table on which the bodies of heads of state often lie in state. On it lay a corpse in funeral garb, its face covered. Around it was a throng of people.

"Who is dead in the White House?" he asked one of the soldiers.

"The President," was his answer. "He was killed by an assassin."

Then came a loud burst of grief from the crowd, which woke him up. According to Lincoln's writings, he was "strangely annoyed" by the dream ever after.

The day that he was assassinated, Lincoln talked about another dream—one that he had had the night before. He was floating on some vast and indistinct expanse or vessel, moving quickly towards the shore, which was also unclear. It was a recurring dream, he said, that he often had before some great event—or disaster.

That afternoon, he stopped to chat with his day guard, William H. Crook. He talked about the fact that some men wanted to kill him, and that, if they did, there was no way to stop them—no matter how diligent and careful those around him were.

At seven p.m., when Crook went off duty and said, "Good night, Mr. President," Lincoln said, "Goodbye, Crook."

A few hours later, the President was dead.

8. NARROW ESCAPES

- Nothing could have stopped the night train—except a strange figure on the tracks.

- Dorothy always watched out for her older brother—even after she died.

- If you meet a procession of the dead in Hawaii, be quick and hide yourself well. Otherwise, you might not live out the night.

Night Train

The night train from London to Birmingham had stopped in the middle of a field. That wasn't unusual. In 1942, with bombings almost every night, you got used to messed-up schedules and unexpected delays. At least, ten-year-old Paul Kuttner was used to it. He was travelling alone—as he often did since his parents had been killed in the war—to visit a friend from boarding school during his summer vacation.

But there didn't seem to be any reason for the train to stop. There were no sounds of planes or sirens.

Paul saw, by the faint blackout glow of the lights on the side of the railroad car, that a couple of trainmen were standing alongside the tracks, looking up ahead.

He walked to one of the train doors, where some passengers had already stepped out on the dark field. They were talking about something on the tracks, up ahead about 50 or 60 feet. It looked like a man in a black cape with his arms stretched out to the sides above his head.

Paul jumped down from the train to look for himself. They were right. The man looked like Dracula.

His arms—were they arms or wings?—in his cape were waving slowly and softly, almost rhythmically. Even with the train's headlights shining on the man, Paul couldn't see his face—or any of his features— just a blackness.

The engineer had been blowing the train's whistle, trying to get the fellow to move, but there was no change in his position or his movements.

It was a warm summer night, but Paul started shivering.

More people were climbing out of the train now. A few of them yelled at the man—or the thing—on the tracks. A soldier gave two warning shots in the air with his rifle. But still the figure gave no indication that he heard them or that he would ever move.

At last, several of the braver passengers began walking up the tracks towards the dark figure. Paul started to go with them, but one of the trainmen pulled him back.

"You stay here, lad," he said, putting a large, firm hand on Paul's shoulder.

As the group approached the figure, some of the passengers screamed. Paul could see them putting their arms out through the darkness. There was nothing there, they were saying. Nothing that they could feel, anyway!

A couple of the passengers walked farther down along the tracks, past where the figure seemed to be. Paul could see them talking and pointing and he could hear their voices getting higher, more excited, but he couldn't hear what they were saying.

The group of passengers was now half walking and half running back to the train, all talking at once.

Because, just beyond the spot where the shadow was, an overpass had been destroyed. If the train had gone just a few hundred feet farther, it would have smashed into the pile of rubble and derailed. Many of the passengers and crew surely would have been killed.

Suddenly, a passenger pointed to the headlight.

"My God! Look at that," the man exclaimed.

And there, pressed against the train's headlight, was a butterfly—either that, Paul thought, or a giant moth. Its wings were spread and moving delicately.

"It's a butterfly that's casting a shadow," the train-man said loudly, very relieved, "just a blooming butterfly!"

The butterfly, blocking some of the light, was casting a blacker shadow on the pile of rubble up ahead—a shadow that looked like a vampire. The waving of the figure's arms were the wing movements of the insect.

Why was no word given to the train company of the wrecked overpass? They found out later that the bombing had just taken place earlier that same night, and no one knew about it yet. Had the train not stopped, they all would have been killed. And, nothing could have stopped the train—except perhaps a "butterfly."

Paul thought a lot about that in the days and years that followed. About what a lucky thing it was that a butterfly had settled on the headlight. And that it didn't just get smashed and die. And that the driver of the train saw that there was something up ahead. And that he stopped in time. And that a few passengers walked ahead and found out about the overpass.

Was all that really luck? Or was it something else?

Still Looking Out for Her Brother

Though she was two years younger than he was, Dorothy was always watching out for her older brother, Bob. She was his biggest fan, his best friend, and also his guardian angel. She would be there whenever he needed help or kind words or someone to talk to or a good laugh. Bob really liked having his little sister around.

Dorothy was about 20 years old when she died suddenly after an operation, but she never stopped helping Bob. The first time was in May 1926. He was standing outside his garage during a thunderstorm, when he heard Dorothy's voice, "Move, Bob, move!"

He quickly stepped away, and the next moment lightning struck the garage door, exactly where he had been standing.

The next time was in December 1942. Bob was in bed when he heard her voice say, "Wake up, Bob."

The house was filled with fumes from a defective stove. Had he gone on sleeping, he surely would have died.

The third time he heard Dorothy's voice was in 1951. He was returning from a trip with his wife, who was in the back seat of the car, and his mother-in-law, who was driving.

It was just beginning to get dark and they were nearing a narrow bridge when a large car sped past them, forcing them way over to the side of the road.

And there was Dorothy's voice, "Grab the wheel, Bob."

He reached over to take the wheel from his mother-in-law, moving his body to the middle of the front seat in order to do it.

The next moment, a steel beam from the bridge, which must have been sticking out, tore open the entire right side of the car, passing right through the place where Bob had been sitting. It ripped open the car, people remarked later, "like a tin can."

"It's great to know that she's still looking out for her big brother," Bob said.

The Night Marchers

George Nawoakoa was a young boy when he saw the marchers. It was on the Hawaiian island of Oahu. He was on his way home from a neighbor's house, and it was getting dark. Suddenly, he saw something strange coming up the hill behind him. It seemed like a cloud of dust, but it shone like silver. There was only a sliver of a moon—not enough to explain all that shining.

He thought it looked like smoke until he saw the people. And then he realized what he was seeing. It was the night marchers—a procession of the dead. He had heard about them. They would come up from the water and climb the hills to a temple or shrine on the clifftops, chanting and beating drums.

It was said that if they caught a glimpse of a living person, one of three things could happen: One, the procession would disappear immediately. Two, the person would drop dead. Three, the dead would kill the living.

George shivered and hid in back of a huge stone on the side of the road.

The people were of all ages, and they looked pale and strange. They took a long time passing by, and they went on up to an old temple in the hills. They didn't see George. And that was the only time he ever saw them.

People on other islands in the Hawaiian group have seen the procession too. One of them claims that the spirits each carry a light. She could almost see their faces in the misty glow.

A tourist on Oahu once saw them as they came from the water in what seemed like canoes or small boats. Each carried a light as they walked along the beach and out towards Diamond Head.

Years ago, children used to be warned to hide from the walking dead in a spot protected from the wind. The idea was to have the wind strike the dead first. Otherwise the scent of the children's bodies would give them away. Then, their only chance would be to have an ancestor among the spirits. Their ancestor could cast a spell over the others, so they could not see the children, and would permit them to live.

One particular woman had not been warned, because her mother did not want to frighten her. But once, when she was about eight years old, she woke up and heard the drums. It seemed as if they were coming from her front yard. She tried to wake up the others who were staying in the house, but they couldn't hear anything and went back to sleep. She ran down to the gate and there she saw a group of people, holding lights in front of them and chanting.

She spoke to them and they stopped. She could feel them gathering around her. Then a man said, "She is one of us. I am her ancestor." No one else said a word. They just turned away slowly and continued on their way up the hill. She walked along with them for a while and then, suddenly, they disappeared.

"I wasn't afraid, either," she said, laughing. "If I had only known what I should have known, I would never have gotten out of bed!"

It is said that only some see the night marchers—those who are *pololei*—right inside.

9. MYSTERIOUS POWERS

- A great mystic predicts his own death—as if it were a lunch date.

- A famous writer fills in a detail of a ghostly story—that he could not possibly have known.

- Psychic to the Third Reich, Hanussen's most startling prediction came true four years after his death.

- Houdini did get through from beyond the grave. What was the message he gave his wife?

Prediction of Death

Emanuel Swedenborg was a world-famous professor, scientist, and mystic, who lived in Sweden more than 200 years ago, eventually founding his own church.

In February 1772, when he was 84 years old, he wrote a letter to John Wesley, the man who established the Methodist Church (and whose family was haunted by a poltergeist; see page 59).

"Sir," he wrote, "I have been informed in the world of spirits that you have a strong desire to converse with me. I shall be happy to see you, if you will favor me with a visit."

It was true: John Wesley *had* been wanting to get together with Swedenborg very much, though he had never mentioned it to anyone.

Wesley wrote back that he was about to leave on a six-month trip, but would get in touch with Swedenborg as soon as he returned.

Swedenborg wrote back promptly. Wesley's plan would not work out, he claimed, because he was going into the world of spirits on the 29th day of the next month, never to return.

Swedenborg died March 29, 1772.

What a Coincidence!

Charles Dickens, the novelist, published a ghost story in a journal called *All the Year Round*. It was a true story that had been told him by a portrait painter friend.

After the story was published, the artist sent Dickens his own account of his experience, and Dickens found it so original—and so different from the account that he himself had written—that his own story paled by comparison.

The artist complained to Dickens that he had been commissioned to write the story for another publication—but when he read Dickens' version in *All the Year Round*, he was shocked. Dickens must have read the story he wrote and used it to write his own version.

"For example," he wrote, "how else is it possible that the date, the 13th of September, could have appeared in your story? I never told the date to anyone until I wrote it."

Dickens' story had originally had no date. But when reading the proofs, he thought it was important that some date be put in. So, he wrote in any day at all— "September 13th"—in the margin.

The Devil's Prophet

Hanussen was a hypnotist, a psychic, and a fabulous showman. He wasn't handsome or impressive-looking, but he was fascinating to watch, and clever enough to know how to put together a compelling performance. When Hitler came to power, he did favors for the Nazi officials, and received favors in return. That's why they called him "the Devil's Prophet."

Like many psychics, Hanussen did have special paranormal abilities, but he couldn't count on them always being there when he needed them. So he cheated. He eventually hired a "secretary," Dzino Ismet, who became his right-hand man. Dzino would "research" important people, so that Hanussen could come up with startling truths and appear all-knowing.

But Hanussen didn't always cheat. He once told a beautiful, elegant baroness that in one month she would leave her husband and go to live with him (Hanussen) and become an assistant in his act. He would eventually leave her, he said, penniless. The baroness could not believe his arrogance in telling her that. When she met him on the street a few weeks later and he reminded her about it, she slapped his face. Hanussen was wrong—on one count. It took two months—not one—for the baroness to succumb to Hanussen's fascination. And it all happened just as he said it would.

At one performance he singled out a distinguished-looking fellow in the audience who was a bank president, and told him that a fire had just started in his bank, caused by a short circuit.

"What are you waiting for?" Hanussen asked him. "You have four minutes to call the fire department, before the fire gets to your safe. Go now and you can salvage something. Call the fire department, man! Why do you hesitate?"

After a few very uncertain seconds, the shaken banker followed an usher to a telephone. Soon fire engines were heard outside the theatre. Hanussen had been right. And there was no way he could have known about a short circuit in the wiring. The contents of the vault were saved just in time.

Hanussen's most chilling prediction was one that was fulfilled after his death.

He had been sitting with Grace Cameron, one of the hostesses at a Berlin dance hall, after one of his performances. She was English and one of the few women who did not find Hanussen irresistible. He liked her and respected her feelings.

Suddenly, Hanussen told her that she would meet the man she was going to marry—right there in the dance hall. He would be tall and handsome and rich—Hanussen's face went dark. "And you must not marry him," he said, "because he will be your murderer!"

A few months later, he was sitting at breakfast when his assistant, Dzino, told him that he was going to get married.

Hanussen was disgusted that the darkly good-looking Dzino—who had grown rich working for Hanussen—would sink to anything so commonplace as marrying.

"And who is the woman?" he asked idly.

"Grace Cameron," Dzino said.

Hanussen spun around. "You can't do that!" he said. "I won't let you!"

And he repeated to Dzino what he had told Grace, adding that after Dzino shot her, he would kill himself.

Dzino didn't believe Hanussen. He knew only too well that Hanussen cheated much of the time. He had often helped him do it. And knowing the way Hanussen went after women, Dzino thought he was probably jealous and wanted Grace for himself.

Grace was more inclined to believe Hanussen, but she was wildly in love with Dzino and didn't want the prediction to be true.

The Nazis eventually turned against Hanussen and shot him to death in a forest near Berlin.

It was four years after that, in 1937, that Dzino Ismet, then an unemployed gambling house worker, shot his wife Grace and their child to death in Vienna and went on to take his own life.

Messages from the Dead

Many people know that Harry Houdini was obsessed, for the latter part of his life, anyway, with finding out if consciousness continues after death. He spent great amounts of time and money testing the mediums he had heard about to see if any were authentic. (Very few didn't resort to trickery at least some of the time.)

And he made a pact with his mother: After she died, she would send him a message that they set up in advance—a message only she, Houdini, and his wife, Bess, knew. That is, she would do it if it were possible.

He made a similar pact with Bess as well. Whichever one died first would send back a message for the other. They devised a different secret message from the one he had set up with his mother—and they told it to no one, so that, were the message to get through, there could be no doubt that it was genuine.

Most people, though, aren't really sure what happened after that. Did he get through or not? What was the message?

This is what happened.

The psychic's name was Arthur Ford. He was not one of the mediums whom Houdini had discredited, but an ordained minister whose reputation was extraordinarily high. At a séance he was holding with a group of friends, Houdini's mother came through, saying that her message would open up the way for that of her son.

Her message started with FORGIVE and then went on to family matters. She instructed Arthur Ford to deliver the message to Bess, who confirmed that it was the one Houdini had waited in vain to hear ever since his mother died. Bess wrote that had he heard it in time, it would probably have changed the course of his life.

Then words from Houdini himself started to come to Ford—one or two at a time—as he did sittings with other people. Eventually, the following message was pieced together:

A man who says he is Harry Houdini, but whose real name is Ehrich Weiss, is here and wishes to send to his wife, Beatrice Houdini, the ten-word code which he agreed to do if it were possible for him to communicate. He says you are to take his message to her and upon acceptance of it, he

wishes her to follow out the plan they agreed upon before his passing. This is the code:
ROSABELLE ** ANSWER ** TELL ** PRAY ** ANSWER ** LOOK ** TELL ** ANSWER ** ANSWER ** TELL

The message went on, telling her to announce the receipt of his message, and not to be disturbed by what people would say. She was to return a code to him—which the two of them alone understood. And then, finally, he would give her the one word that he wanted to send back.

The next day, two members of the group who had been present at the sitting—one of them the associate editor of the *Scientific American*—went to see Bess and deliver the message from her husband.

"It is right!" she said, filled with emotion.

She invited Ford to come to her house the next day. After he went into a trance, the meeting went like this:

FORD: He tells you to take off your wedding
      ring and tell them what Rosabelle means.
BESS *(taking off her ring and singing):*
      Rosabelle, sweet Rosabelle,
      I love you more than I can tell;
      O'er me you cast a spell,
      I love you, my Rosabelle!
FORD: He says, "I thank you, darling. The first
      time I heard you sing that song was in
      our first show together years ago."

Houdini went on to give a much longer message—a

very excited and enthusiastic one—about survival after death and how he wanted to let everyone know about it. If you want to read the other things he said, the book that tells it all is Arthur Ford's biography, *Nothing So Strange*.

After that the code was explained:

ANSWER	B
TELL	E
PRAY, ANSWER	L
LOOK	I
TELL	E
ANSWER, ANSWER	V
TELL	E

Houdini's message was:

ROSABELLE, BELIEVE.

Acknowledgments

With deepest thanks to my friends Glen Vecchione and Paul Kuttner, for sharing their extraordinary experiences, relating them so splendidly that all I had to do was take them down, and for giving me permission to publish them in this book.

Also thanks to my dear friend Peter Amann-Wein for his suggestions—especially for introducing me to Dudleytown.

INDEX

African Transvaal, 28
All the Year Round, 87
Ashmore, Charles, 6–7
A.T. Lacey, 74

Ballaculish, Scotland, 69–70
Beresford, Lady, 70
Birds, white, 51
Blackfeet tribe, 64
Boulton family, 69–70
Brakeman, ghost of, 42–43
Brophy, Patrick, 17
Brothers and sisters, 13–14, 34–36, 81–82
Brown, Henry Armitt, 71–72
Bullet that waited, 66
Burnside, Harry, 28–30
Butterfly, 80

Cabin cruiser, 40–41
Cameron, Grace, 89–90
Carpenter, Constance, 57–58
Casket, unburied, 68
Cheney, Mary, 17
Citron, Henry, 56
Clark, William C., 17
Clemens, Henry, 73–74
Clinton, Ohio, 42
Cree, massacre of the, 62–65
Crombie, Dorothy, 23–24
Crook, William H., 76
Curses and jinxes, 15–30

Dead, procession of, 83
Denny, Cecil A., 62–65
Diamond Head, Oahu, 84
Dickens, Charles, 87
Disappearance, 6–7
Dog, black, 46–48
Dreams, 67–76
Dudleytown, 16–18

Earrings, greenstone, 22–24

Ford, Arthur, 92–94
Fort Walsh, Canada, 62
Fundudzi, Lake, 28–30

Gallipoli, Turkey, 66
Greeley, Horace, 17
Halberstern, Capt. Albrecht, 19
Hanging Hills, 46–48
Hannussen, 88–90
Hawkins, Reverend, 11
Houdini, Harry, 91–94

Ismet, Dzino, 88–90

Jackson, Mississippi, 9
Jeffrey, 59–60

Kuttner, Paul, 78–80

Lillie, Beatrice, 57–58
Lincoln, Abraham, 75–76
London, England, 78
Lovecraft, H.P., 32
Luck changer, 22

Makinson, John Russell, 66
Maori tradition, 22–24
Massey, Dorothy and Raymond, 49–50
Meriden, Connecticut, 47
Mice, 49–50
Monroe family, 37–39

Name, lucky, 12
Nawoakoa, George, 83–84
New Orleans, Louisiana, 54
New York, New York, 49–50, 71–72
Nothing So Strange, 94

Oahu, Hawaii, 83
Oldman River, Canada, 62–65
Oshkosh Northwestern, 39
Owensville, Indiana, 65
Owlsbury, 16–18
Oxenham family, 51–52

Palm Beach Playhouse, Florida, 57
Pearl Harbor, 65
Pennsylvania, 74
Plate-throwing poltergeist, 54–56
Poltergeists, 53–60

Prayer meeting, 9–11
Pynchon, W.H.C., 47
Python, spirit of, 28

Quilt, haunted, 37–39
Quincy, Illinois, 6

Reenactment, 62–65
Richter, Second Lieutenant, 26
Ring: turquoise, 19; wedding, 9
Roca, Nelly, 54–56
Room, screaming, 34–36
Rotorua, New Zealand, 22–24

St. Louis, Missouri, 73–74
Saugasso, Robert, 21
Scientific American, 93
Seagrave Observatory, Rhode Island, 32–33
Sheepshead Bay marina, 40–41
Shipwrecks, 12
Sisters and brothers, 13–14, 34–36, 81–82
Skyscrapers Club, 32
Sussex, England, 34
Swedenborg, Emanuel, 86
Swift, General Herman, 17

Tapu, 22
Thacker, William, 29–30
Train, night, 78–80
Twain, Mark, 73–74
Twins, time, 8

U-boat 65, 25
Umberto I, King, 8

Valentine's Day, 13
Van Blerk, Hendrik and Jacobus, 28
Voodoo, 56

Wedding ring, 9–11
Weichter, Kurt, 20
Weiss, Ehrich, 92
Wesley: family, 59–60; John, 86
Williams, Hugh, 12